THE STORY OF THE
PITTSBURGH PIRATES

Published by Creative Education
P.O. Box 227, Mankato, Minnesota 56002
Creative Education is an imprint of The Creative Company

Design and production by Blue Design
Printed in the United States of America

Photographs by Corbis (Bettmann), Getty Images (Al Bello, Bruce Bennett Studios, Diamond Images, Elsa, Focus on Sport, Paul Jaslenski, Kidwiler Collection/Diamond Images, Jonathan Kirn/All, MLB Photos, National Baseball Hall of Fame Library/MLB Photos, Rich Pilling/MLB Photos, Art Rickerby//Time Life Pictures, Mark Rucker/Transcendental Graphics, Jamie Squire, Rick Stewart)

Library of Congress Cataloging-in-Publication Data

Goodman, Michael E.
The story of the Pittsburgh Pirates / by Michael E. Goodman.
p. cm. — (Baseball: the great American game)
Includes index.
ISBN-13: 978-1-58341-498-9
1. Pittsburgh Pirates (Baseball team)—History—Juvenile literature. I. Title. II. Series.

GV875.P5.G66 2007
796.357'640974886—dc22   2006027464

First Edition
9 8 7 6 5 4 3 2 1

Cover: Outfielder Roberto Clemente
Page 1: Catcher Tony Peña
Page 3: Pitcher Ian Snell

THE STORY OF THE
PITTSBURGH
PIRATES

by Michael E. Goodman

WILLIE STARGELL

THE STORY OF THE
Pittsburgh Pirates

I t's the sixth inning of Game 7 of the 1979 World Series, and the Pittsburgh Pirates are behind again. That's nothing new in this series. The Pirates have already bounced back from a three-games-to-one deficit against the Baltimore Orioles to tie the se-ries and reach this seventh game.

Now, they are trailing Baltimore 1–0 in a tense pitcher's duel. Veteran first baseman Willie Stargell strides to the plate with a runner on first. "Pops" has been the Pirates' best clutch performer all year, and the team could use his firepower now. Stargell twirls his bat around in the batter's box and eyes Orioles pitcher Scott McGregor. On the second pitch, McGregor tries to slip a slider past Stargell, but Pops sends it soaring high above the right-field fence to put Pittsburgh ahead, 2–1. Three innings later, the Pirates' amazing comeback is complete, and they are world champions for the fifth time.

PROUD PIRATES

In the 1740s, French traders and soldiers established a trading post and fort where the Allegheny and Monongahela Rivers meet to form the Ohio River. In 1758, British troops captured that fort during the French and Indian War and renamed it Fort Pitt in honor of British prime minister William Pitt. Settlers soon established a town called Pittsburgh around the fort. The availability of hydroelectric power and large iron ore reserves in western Pennsylvania helped Pittsburgh grow to become the steelmaking center of the United States by the late 1800s. It took strong, determined people to work in steel mills, and the city quickly became known for its work ethic.

Hard work and determination also became trademarks of the city's professional baseball team, the Pittsburgh Pirates, which joined the National League (NL) in 1888. The club was originally called the Alleghenies but received a different name in 1891 after a dispute with a rival American Association team in Philadelphia called the Athletics. The Alleghenies had signed the Athletics' gifted second baseman, Lou Bierbauer, and the furious Athletics protested loudly. "You've stolen one of our best players. You're no better

Honus Wagner was fiercely loyal to Pittsburgh, rejecting larger contracts elsewhere to stay in the "Steel City."

THE FIRST WORLD SERIES

When Pittsburgh Pirates owner Barney Dreyfuss proposed holding the first World Series after the 1903 season, he primarily had business interests in mind. In his letter to the owner of the Boston Pilgrims, Dreyfuss wrote that a championship competition "would create great interest in baseball, in our leagues, and in our players. I also believe it would be a financial success." Dreyfuss was right. Overflow crowds came to each game in the series, benefiting the owners as well as scalpers, who bought large blocks of tickets for as little as $1 each and resold them for $5 to $10 on the street.

Every seat was filled for each game, and hundreds of fans stood in the back of the outfield. A rule was made that any ball hit into the crowd on the field would be an automatic triple. The teams combined for 25 triples in the series, which is still a record. The owners also agreed to share their profits from the gate receipts with the players—a practice that is still followed today. The winning Pilgrims received checks for $1,182 each for their victorious efforts. In comparison, following the 2005 World Series, each member of the victorious Chicago White Sox earned $324,000.

than pirates!" Philadelphia team leaders cried. Alleghenies management decided to keep not only the player but the new name as well. From then on, the team was known as the Pittsburgh Pirates.

Even with its "pirated" player, Pittsburgh remained near the bottom of the league throughout the 1890s. Then, starting in 1900, a group of outstanding new players arrived in Pittsburgh and transformed the Pirates into a powerhouse. From 1901 to 1903, the Pirates captured three straight NL pennants.

Leading the way on those great teams were pitcher Charles "Deacon" Phillippe, outfielder/manager Fred Clarke, and the "Flying Dutchman"—shortstop Honus Wagner. Wagner soon established himself as the best all-around player in the league. The broad-shouldered infielder had bowed legs that made him appear unathletic, but he was an outstanding batter and fielder. As one reporter wrote, "He walks like a crab, fields like an octopus, and hits like the devil." During the first decade of the 20th century, Wagner led the NL in batting average eight times and in stolen bases five times while playing flawlessly in the field. "He was the greatest shortstop ever—the greatest everything ever," said Pirates third baseman Tommy Leach.

After the team's third straight NL championship, club president Barney Dreyfuss sent a letter to the owner of the American League (AL) champs, the

A fiery competitor, early star Fred Clarke helped Pittsburgh win the 1901, 1902, and 1903 NL pennants.

Boston Pilgrims, suggesting that the two clubs square off in a best-of-nine series for the right to be called world champions. The Boston owner accepted the challenge, and baseball's first World Series became a reality. Phillippe twice outdueled Boston ace Cy Young during the series, but the Pilgrims came out on top, five games to three.

In 1909, Pittsburgh returned to the World Series after winning a club-record 110 games. The series that year was billed as a marquee matchup between Wagner and Detroit Tigers outfielder Ty Cobb, the AL's best hitter. But the real star turned out to be Pirates rookie Charles "Babe" Adams, who pitched three complete-game victories to lead the Pirates to a four-games-to-three series triumph and their first world championship.

PITCHER · # WILBUR COOPER

Left-handed Wilbur Cooper won 202 games in a Pirates uniform, more than any other pitcher in team history. Cooper had great control and was a fast worker on the mound, but his sidearm delivery seemed so effortless that some fans thought he wasn't working hard at all. "Nothing could be further from the truth," wrote one reporter. "The Pirates southpaw works as hard as any other hurler, but his grace and ease of motion mislead some of the rooters." Cooper was also known for his fielding skill and a devastating pick-off move to third base that often nailed unsuspecting runners.

STATS

Pirates seasons: 1912–24

Height: 5-11

Weight: 175

- **216–178 career record**

- **4 seasons of 20-plus wins**

- **279 career complete games**

- **2.89 career ERA**

| WILBUR COOPER | PITTSBURGH |
| PITCHER | PIRATES |

Paul (left) and Lloyd Waner (right) each spent 15 seasons with the Pirates. Paul was three years the elder.

PAUL & LLYOD WANER

PIE AND POISON

fter that 1909 championship run, the Pirates slowly faded in the NL standings. The great players of the pennant-winning teams got older and slower. It would take club management several years to build a big winner again. Pittsburgh's fortunes finally began to change for the better in the early 1920s with the arrival of third baseman Harold "Pie" Traynor. An outstanding all-around player, Traynor was equally skilled at the plate and in the field. "He had the quickest hands and the quickest arms of any third baseman I ever saw," said Pirates first baseman Charlie Grimm.

Traynor solidified the Pirates' defense and joined with speedy outfielders Kiki Cuyler and Max Carey to give Pittsburgh the top offensive attack in the league. In 1925, the Pirates raced to the top of the NL, leading the league in runs scored, hits, doubles, triples, and stolen bases. The club won 95 games to capture the pennant.

The Pirates got off to a slow start in the World Series against the Washington Senators, losing three of the first four games. Then they stormed

PIE TRAYNOR

back with two straight wins to even the series. In Game 7, Pittsburgh fell behind again before rallying in the eighth inning against Washington's Hall of Fame pitcher Walter Johnson to capture the championship.

O ver the next two seasons, Traynor was joined in Pittsburgh by a pair of hard-hitting outfielders—the Waner brothers. As a rookie in 1926, right fielder Paul Waner did two important things for the Pirates. He led the team in batting with a .336 average, and he told the team owner, "My younger brother Lloyd is an even better player than I am. You'd better grab him." Luckily, the Pirates took his advice. For the next decade, the Waner brothers were the heart of the Pittsburgh offense. They earned the nicknames "Big Poison" and "Little Poison" because they were murder on opposing pitchers, and each was later inducted into the Hall of Fame.

Pie and the Poisons led the Pirates to another pennant in 1927, but Pittsburgh was no match for the New York Yankees' "Murderers' Row" lineup in the World Series. Some writers claimed the Pirates became intimidated even before the first pitch was thrown, watching Babe Ruth and other Yankees sluggers slam ball after ball out of the park during batting practice. The Yankees swept the series in four games.

ALL-TIME TEAM

CATCHER · TONY PEÑA

When they were growing up in the Dominican Republic, Tony Peña and his brother Ramón, a minor-league pitcher in the Pirates organization, learned to play baseball from their mother, a former softball star. She taught Tony to set up behind the plate in an unusual crouch with one leg extended to the side. From that position, Peña was able to block wild pitches effectively and to rise up quickly to throw out would-be base stealers. Tony's fielding skills and timely hitting helped him become a five-time All-Star. After his playing career, he managed the Kansas City Royals for four seasons.

TONY PEÑA
CATCHER

PITTSBURGH
PIRATES

STATS

Pirates seasons: 1980–86

Height: 6-0

Weight: 180

- **708 career RBI**

- **5-time All-Star**

- **4-time Gold Glove winner**

- **11,212 career putouts**

FIRST BASEMAN · WILLIE STARGELL

Pirates manager Chuck Tanner once said, "When you had Willie Stargell on your team, it was like having a 10-karat diamond on your finger." With his talent and leadership, "Pops" was the Pirates' most valuable player on and off the field. Stargell was a scary presence at the plate. He would twirl his heavy bat in a sweeping windmill motion before settling in to face the pitcher. Then he would stride powerfully into the pitch and send the ball soaring high and far. A 12-foot-high statue of Stargell today stands outside PNC Park, befitting a man who often seemed much larger than life.

WILLIE STARGELL
FIRST BASEMAN

PITTSBURGH
PIRATES

STATS

Pirates seasons: 1962–82

Height: 6-2

Weight: 225

- **475 career HR**

- **1979 NL co-MVP**

- **7-time All-Star**

- **Baseball Hall of Fame inductee (1988)**

The Pirates stayed near the top of the NL throughout the rest of the 1920s and '30s, but they never finished higher than second place. Pittsburgh fans longed for another championship, but they settled for watching some talented offensive stars perform in the Steel City. Among the best of those players was shortstop Arky Vaughn, who arrived in 1932 and batted over .300 in each of his 10 seasons in Pittsburgh black-and-gold.

Even with all of their offensive talent, the Pirates fell short year after year. "Gee that was tough to take," Paul Waner said later. "We had good teams, too. You know, Pie, Arky, and me and Lloyd—all good players. But we never quite made it. It'd just tear you apart."

DERAILING THE BIG TRAIN

The 1925 World Series was billed as a battle between the best-hitting team in the NL—the Pirates—and arguably the best pitcher in AL history, Walter Johnson of the Washington Senators. The Pirates' starting lineup had batted an amazing .324 in 1925, while Johnson, known as "The Big Train" because of his locomotive-like fastball, had been a 20-game winner for the 12th time in his career. Johnson shut down the Pirates' bats completely in Games 1 and 4, holding Pittsburgh to 1 run and 11 hits altogether. The Pirates battled back to win Games 5 and 6 but faced two major hurdles going into Game 7. For one thing, no team had ever come back from a three-games-to-one deficit to win a World Series before. And for another, they would be facing Johnson again. When the Senators got off to a 4–0 lead in the top of the first inning, Pirates fans feared the worst. But Johnson didn't have his best stuff, and the Pirates trailed only 7–6 when they batted in the bottom of the eighth. Pittsburgh then capitalized on sloppy Senators fielding to score three unearned runs against Johnson and clinch its second world championship.

PIRATE POWER

During the 1940s, the Pirates were an average team with one real star—slugging outfielder Ralph Kiner, who won the NL home run crown a record seven seasons in a row. But even Kiner couldn't keep the team from spiraling downhill during the early 1950s. The Pirates lost more than 100 games each year in 1952, 1953, and 1954 and finished dead last in the NL all three seasons.

Pittsburgh fans were upset, but general manager Branch Rickey had a plan in mind for rebuilding the club. He began trading away veterans and bringing in talented young players such as shortstop Dick Groat, relief pitcher Elroy Face, and slugging first baseman Dick Stuart, whose fielding difficulties earned him the nickname "Dr. Strangeglove." In a final brilliant move before the 1955 season, Rickey signed a young Puerto Rican outfielder named Roberto Clemente away from the Brooklyn Dodgers. Clemente would become the Pirates' shining star for the next 18 years.

Rickey's rebuilding plan took longer than he expected, but by 1960, all the pieces were in place for Pittsburgh to make another NL pennant run. During that magical season, everything seemed to go right for the Pirates: The team

Longtime star Roberto Clemente ran the bases with hustle and daring, scoring 1,416 runs in his career.

DICK GROAT

ALMOST PERFECT

On May 26, 1959, Pirates left-hander Harvey Haddix pitched the best game ever thrown in major-league history—and lost. Haddix had everything going right against the Milwaukee Braves that night. In the clubhouse before the game, Haddix had discussed how he planned to pitch to each Braves batter. Third baseman Don Hoak predicted, "Harv, if you pitch the way you say you will, you'll have a no-hitter." After nine innings, Haddix was doing even better than that; he was hurling a perfect game. Twenty-seven Braves batters had come to the plate, and all had made outs. But the game still wasn't over, because the Pirates hadn't scored yet either. With two outs in the top of the 10th, Pittsburgh first baseman Dick Stuart hit a shot that looked like it would clear the fence, but the wind held it up for a long out. If Haddix was upset, he didn't show it. He just kept mowing down the Braves in order in the 10th, 11th, and 12th innings. Then, in the bottom of the 13th, a Hoak throwing error ended the perfect game. That runner later scored, giving Milwaukee a 1–0 win. For Harvey Haddix, being almost perfect wasn't good enough.

Vernon Law rarely overpowered hitters during his great 1960 season, instead baffling them with his pinpoint control.

compiled a 95–59 record, third-best in club history, to capture its first NL title in 33 years; Groat was named league Most Valuable Player (MVP); Clemente batted a solid .316; and pitcher Vernon Law earned the NL Cy Young Award as the league's best pitcher with a 20–9 record.

The glue holding the team together, however, was second baseman Bill Mazeroski. "Maz" was a natural leader and a steadying influence on the rest of the players. He was also one of the finest-fielding second-sackers of all time. Describing how Mazeroski handled the pivot on a double play, Dick Groat said, "It was as if his hands never touched the ball. As soon as the ball touched his glove, it was on its way to first base. Frankly, I never saw anything like it."

Maz earned a lasting spot in Pittsburgh history for his performance in the 1960 World Series against the New York Yankees. The battle between the league champs came down to the bottom of the ninth inning of Game 7 with

BILL MAZEROSKI

Bill Mazeroski's walk-off, World Series-clinching home run in 1960 instantly made him part of baseball legend.

the teams tied 9–9. Maz led off for the Pirates and tried to relax at the plate. "On my previous at bat, I had overswung and grounded out," he recalled. "I wanted to make certain I didn't do the same thing again." Maz took one pitch for a ball. Then he slammed the next one over the left-field wall to secure the championship for the Pirates. Outside Pittsburgh's Forbes Field, cars honked, trolley cars clanged, and excited Pirates fans danced in the streets, celebrating the victory.

CLEMENTE AND "POPS"

ittsburgh's time at the top was short-lived. The next year, the Pirates fell to a disappointing sixth place and remained in the middle of the league standings throughout most of the 1960s. First baseman and future team captain Willie Stargell, who joined the Pirates in 1962, said, "The spark had disappeared from the club . . . the magic had passed. All that remained were 25 talented ballplayers not good enough to win a pennant."

The most talented player of the group—and the most misunderstood—was Roberto Clemente. A man of great pride and honesty, Clemente felt he never received the respect he deserved because he was Latin American and had dif-

Willie Stargell was merely average as a fielder but earned wide renown for his colorful personality and slugging power.

WILLIE STARGELL

SECOND BASEMAN · BILL MAZEROSKI

Some baseball experts consider Bill Mazeroski the best-fielding second baseman of all time. His quick hands enabled him to establish a major-league career record for turning double plays (1,706). He is even more famous for the clutch home run he hit to win the 1960 World Series. But "Maz" brought something special to the Pirates that went beyond batting or fielding. Said Pirates pitcher Steve Blass: "They can talk about all the great Pirates—and there have been a lot of them. But Maz represented the spirit of Pittsburgh and the Pirates better than any of them."

STATS

Pirates seasons: 1956–72

Height: 5-11

Weight: 183

- **2,016 career hits**
- **8-time Gold Glove winner**
- **7-time All-Star**
- **Baseball Hall of Fame inductee (2001)**

BILL MAZEROSKI
SECOND BASEMAN

PITTSBURGH
PIRATES

ficulty speaking English. There was no denying his skill on the field, however. During his career in Pittsburgh, Clemente compiled a lifetime batting average of .317 and earned 12 consecutive Gold Gloves for his outstanding fielding.

Clemente saved his best performance for the 1971 World Series, when the reinvigorated Pirates took on and defeated the Baltimore Orioles. With fans all around the country watching him on television, Clemente batted .414 in the series, made several spectacular catches in the field, ran the bases with abandon, and was the unanimous choice as series MVP.

Sadly, that was one of Clemente's last shining moments. In December 1972, he died in a plane crash on his way to deliver medicine and supplies to victims of a terrible earthquake in Nicaragua. At his funeral, the governor of Puerto Rico said, "Our youth lose an idol. Our people lose one of their glories."

With Clemente gone, the mantle of team leadership passed to Willie Stargell. Stargell inspired his teammates with his hard work and sense of humor. He made a special point of "adopting" younger players such as out-fielders Dave Parker and Al Oliver and third baseman Bill Madlock, earning him the nickname "Pops." Pops Stargell created a close-knit Pirates family that started to win big again in the late 1970s. In 1979, the Pirates rose all the way to the top.

That year, Stargell chose a theme song for the team, a disco tune called "We Are Family," and asked that it be played at all home games in Three Rivers Stadium. "That song not only brought us and the fans closer together," Stargell recalled, "but it became a rallying cry for the city as well. We were all one. . . . Pittsburghers all moved to the same beat."

That beat was a winning one. The Pirates edged by the Montreal Expos for the NL Eastern Division crown during the regular season. (The league had been split into two divisions in 1969.) Then they swept the Cincinnati Reds in the NL Championship Series (NLCS) to earn a spot in the World Series against the Baltimore Orioles, the team they had defeated in 1971. Just as in 1971, the series went a full seven games. In the finale, Pops Stargell pounded four hits, including a go-ahead homer, to lead his family to victory.

A FAMILY WIN

The 1979 Pirates were a real family. It was more than just the song that played when the team took the field at Three Rivers Stadium—"We Are Family." They kidded with each other, ate meals together, and gave each other nicknames, such as "Scrap Iron" (second baseman Phil Garner), "Crazy Horse" (shortstop Tim Foli), "Rubber Band Man" (reliever Kent Tekulve), and "Pops" (first baseman Willie Stargell). "These guys would agitate each other before a game," recalled manager Chuck Tanner. "But a family gets together when you go to battle, and that is exactly what we did." In the World Series that year, the Pirates fell behind the Baltimore Orioles three games to one. After Game 4, Tanner learned that his ailing mother had died. His father urged him to stay with the team, however, and manage them to victory. When outfielder Dave Parker, his mom's favorite player, hit a long RBI double to push the Pirates ahead in Game 5, Tanner believed his mother's spirit was inspiring the team. Whatever was behind the turnaround, family power did take over in the final three games, as the Pirates roared back to win the series.

THIRD BASEMAN · PIE TRAYNOR

Harold "Pie" Traynor was one of baseball's finest fielders at third base. He had great reflexes and made an art of diving for balls to his right to stop sure base hits and then firing throws across the diamond to first. A Pittsburgh sportswriter once reported, "The batter doubled down the left-field foul line, but Traynor threw him out." Traynor was an outstanding hitter as well, and his .320 lifetime batting average is the best ever by a third-sacker. Traynor almost always put the ball in play, striking out an average of only 16 times per year during his career.

PIE TRAYNOR
THIRD BASEMAN

PITTSBURGH
PIRATES

STATS

Pirates seasons: 1920–37

Height: 6-0

Weight: 170

• **1,273 career RBI**

• **.320 career BA**

• **10 seasons batting over .300**

• **Baseball Hall of Fame inductee (1948)**

BARRY AND BOBBY

I n the early 1980s, the family broke up. Stargell retired, and most of the other stars moved on to new teams. The Pirates fell to the bottom of the NL East by 1984, but luckily, help was on the way. General manager Syd Thrift promoted two young outfielders, Barry Bonds and Bobby Bonilla, from the club's minor-league farm system in 1986. Then he made some wily trades for pitchers Doug Drabek and Neal Heaton. Thrift asked Pittsburgh fans to be patient while these young players developed.

The fans' patience was soon rewarded. In 1988, the Pirates surprised most people by making a strong run for the division title before losing out to the New York Mets late in the season. The club suffered through injuries in 1989 but was back and better than ever in 1990. This time the Pirates caught and then passed the Mets in September to win the NL East crown. The Pirates were hot, but they couldn't match the scorching Cincinnati Reds in the NLCS. The Reds topped Pittsburgh in six games and then swept the powerful Oakland A's in the World Series.

Despite the loss in the playoffs, Pirates fans were thrilled by how the club had performed in 1990. Bonds had earned the league MVP trophy by batting

Barry Bonds became one of the 1990s' best all-around players, a superb hitter, speedy runner, and defensive dynamo.

BARRY BONDS

SHORTSTOP · HONUS WAGNER

John Peter "Honus" Wagner spent 57 years in a Pirates uniform—18 as a player and 39 as a coach. He was the team's first great star and still holds club records for doubles, triples, and runs scored. Wagner earned the nickname "The Flying Dutchman" because of his speed on the bases and his German heritage. He had huge hands and sometimes scooped up dirt and rocks along with the ball and threw them all toward first base for the out. Wagner was among five players elected to the Hall of Fame in its first year of existence.

STATS

Pirates seasons: 1900–17

Height: 5-11

Weight: 200

- **3,415 career hits**

- **252 career triples**

- **8-time NL leader in BA**

- **Baseball Hall of Fame inductee (1936)**

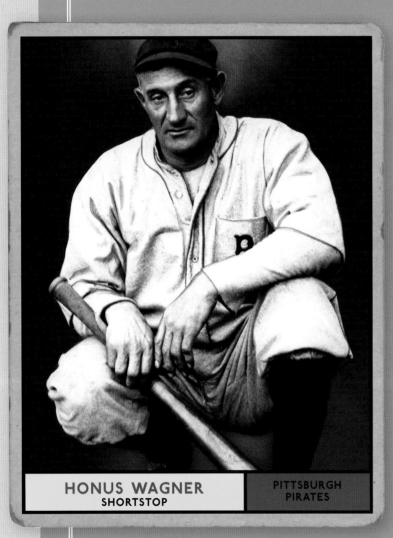

HONUS WAGNER
SHORTSTOP

PITTSBURGH
PIRATES

THE "OUTFIELD OF DREAMS"

In 1989, a baseball movie called *Field of Dreams* was big at the box office. That year, Pirates manager Jim Leyland put together what became known in Pittsburgh as the "Outfield of Dreams"—Barry Bonds in left, Andy van Slyke in center, and Bobby Bonilla in right. No NL team could match the Pirates' trio in the field or at bat. All three made All-Star teams while playing in Pittsburgh. They powered the Pirates to NL East titles in both 1990 and 1991, smacking a combined 142 home runs and driving in 610 runs during the two seasons. Bonds and van Slyke also garnered Gold Glove awards both years for their fielding, and Bonds and Bonilla ranked first and second in the voting for NL MVP in 1990. "I wish I could split the award and give half to Bobby," Bonds said at his award ceremony that year. "He's just as much an MVP as I am." But as good as they were during the regular season, the dream outfielders seemed to fizzle in the playoffs. Their inability to get big hits during NLCS games proved to be a nightmare for Pirates fans.

PIRATES

An All-Star in four of his five full Pirates seasons, Bobby Bonilla helped Pittsburgh win two NL East crowns.

.301 and compiling 33 homers, 114 runs batted in (RBI), and 52 stolen bases. Bonilla had been close behind in the MVP voting, and Drabek had won the Cy Young Award, going 22–6 while walking only 56 batters in his 33 starts.

The Pirates won a second consecutive NL East title in 1991, but they came up short once again in the NLCS, losing to the Atlanta Braves in a tight seven-game series. The same two NL clubs repeated as division champs in 1992 and faced off in another dramatic NLCS. This time, the turning point was a three-run Atlanta rally in the bottom of the ninth inning of Game 7 that crushed Pirates fans' dreams of the pennant. "We were so close," said dejected Pirates shortstop Jay Bell. "I really can't believe it happened still."

The loss to the Braves was devastating for the Pittsburgh organization. The team had already lost Bonilla to free agency in 1991. Shortly after the 1992 postseason, the cash-poor Pirates were unable to match contracts offered to Bonds and Drabek by other teams. With its lineup suddenly depleted, the Pirates dropped quickly in the NL East. A promising era in Pittsburgh baseball had come to an end.

LEFT FIELDER · RALPH KINER

No player except Babe Ruth ever dominated home-run hitting the way Ralph Kiner did from 1946 to 1952: he led the league in homers (or tied for it) his first seven seasons in Pittsburgh. Kiner hit home runs in streaks, once clubbing eight in a four-game span. Unfortunately, he was the Pirates' only offensive weapon during the late 1940s. Once, when Kiner threatened to hold out for more money, the Pirates owner told him, "We finished last with you in the lineup. How much worse could we do without you?" After his playing days, Kiner spent many years as an announcer with the New York Mets.

RALPH KINER
LEFT FIELDER

PITTSBURGH
PIRATES

STATS

Pirates seasons: 1946–53

Height: 6-2

Weight: 195

- **369 career HR**

- **1,015 career RBI**

- **6-time All-Star**

- **Baseball Hall of Fame inductee (1975)**

Tony Womack was a base-stealing terror, leading the league in thefts in both 1997 (60) and 1998 (58).

TONY WOMACK

NEW STADIUM, NEW ERA

ins were hard to come by in Pittsburgh during the rest of the 1990s. As the team declined in the standings, attendance also decreased at Three Rivers Stadium, and an unfortunate cycle took hold. Lower attendance meant less money to spend to sign or develop players who could improve the team's performance on the field. Things got so bad that there was even talk of moving the Pirates from Pittsburgh to northern Virginia. Luckily, in February 1996, newspaper mogul Kevin McClatchy bought the team. He vowed to keep the franchise in Pittsburgh and to help it become competitive again.

Inspired by the new owner's confidence, the Pirates made a strong run in 1997. Led by speedy second baseman Tony Womack, veteran outfielder Al Martin, and tough-as-nails catcher Jason Kendall, the Pirates battled for the NL Central Division lead all season and finished in second place at a surprising 79–83. "A lot of people said we would be a joke," said Womack. "But if we can keep this group of guys together and add another bat or two, we'll be doing the laughing."

Unfortunately, injuries and continuing financial problems made keeping the team together impossible. But McClatchy had another idea that could re-

ELUSIVE HONOR

Over the years, Pirates stars have won a wide variety of honors—MVP awards, Gold Gloves, and Cy Young Awards. But, before 2004, no Pirates newcomer had ever been named NL Rookie of the Year. Then outfielder Jason Bay captured the 2004 award by hitting .282 with 26 homers and 82 RBI. Bay had the double distinction of also being the first Canadian-born player to receive the honor. "The award means the world to me," Bay said. "You walk into the locker room here and see all those jerseys [of past Pirates greats] hanging up. It's kind of amazing it never happened before." Why had the award eluded so many Pirates stars of earlier eras? It was first presented in 1947, so players such as Honus Wagner, Pie Traynor, and Paul Waner could not have won. Even Ralph Kiner, who led the NL in homers during his rookie season in 1946, started his career a year too early. In 1955, Roberto Clemente lost out to St. Louis Cardinals rookie Bill Virdon, who later played center field next to Clemente in the Pittsburgh outfield. In 1963, Willie Stargell finished behind Pete Rose of the Cincinnati Reds, and in 1986, Barry Bonds came in sixth in the voting.

JASON BAY

CENTER FIELDER · MAX CAREY

It was said that the only thing that covered more grass in center field of Pittsburgh's Forbes Field than Max Carey was the smoke from the local steel mills. Carey set league records for putouts and assists by an outfielder, and while he may have been only a better-than-average hitter, he was absolute lightning on the base paths. Carey was one of the heroes for the Pirates in the 1925 World Series when, despite suffering from a broken rib, he batted .436, stole three bases, and got four hits off of Washington Senators ace Walter Johnson in the deciding Game 7.

STATS

Pirates seasons: 1910–26

Height: 5-11

Weight: 170

- **2,665 career hits**
- **738 stolen bases**
- **10-time NL leader in steals**
- **Baseball Hall of Fame inductee (1961)**

MAX CAREY
CENTER FIELDER

PITTSBURGH
PIRATES

JACK WILSON

JACK WILSON – Entering Pittsburgh's lineup in 2001, Wilson quickly proved himself a valuable addition both in the field and at the plate. The wiry infielder was a sound defensive stopper and won a 2004 Silver Slugger award as the NL's top-hitting shortstop.

vitalize the club and its fans as the new millennium approached. In April 1999, construction began on a stadium that would be called PNC Park. Two years later, the Pirates moved into their new home—one of the most beautiful in all of major league baseball. More than 2.4 million fans filled up PNC Park in 2001, thrilled by its dramatic views of the expanding Pittsburgh skyline and the reminders of past Pirates' glory placed all around the stadium—statues of Honus Wagner, Roberto Clemente, and Willie Stargell; newspaper headlines of great moments in team history; and tapestries showing reproductions of baseball cards of legendary Pirates players.

The stadium delighted fans, but the lingering question was whether the team playing in it would be exciting too. General manager Dave Littlefield answered that affirmatively by engineering several key trades starting in 2001. By 2006, the Pirates had assembled a promising collection of talent that included pitchers Zach Duke and Ian Snell, All-Star outfielder Jason Bay, young catcher Ronny Paulino, and third baseman Freddy Sanchez, who won the 2006 NL batting title with a .344 average. The team ended 2006 in the NL Central basement, but the Pirates were confident that they would end a 14-year drought by breaking the .500 mark in 2007. "It's going to be a pretty good year," said Snell before the 2007 season. "This year, we're going to win some games. I guarantee it."

RIGHT FIELDER · ROBERTO CLEMENTE

Roberto Clemente could turn any pitch—even ones at ankle height or nearly over his head—into a base hit. He was a free swinger who nearly always made contact with the ball. Clemente was also the best right fielder of his era, with a rocket arm that struck fear into base runners. But he is perhaps best known for his humanitarian efforts off the field, including the charity mission to Nicaragua that cost him his life. Clemente once said, "Anytime you have an opportunity to make a difference in this world and you don't, then you are wasting your time on Earth."

ROBERTO CLEMENTE
RIGHT FIELDER

PITTSBURGH
PIRATES

STATS

Pirates seasons: 1955–72

Height: 5-11

Weight: 175

- **1,305 career RBI**

- **3,000 career hits**

- **12-time All-Star**

- **Baseball Hall of Fame inductee (1973)**

Pittsburgh was able to show off its new, classically designed PNC Park as the host of the 2006 All-Star Game.

For Pittsburgh fans who had feared losing their franchise just a few years before, the improved lineup and new stadium provided a promise that baseball would continue to flourish in the Steel City for many years to come. Pirates great Willie Stargell once said, "Pittsburgh isn't fancy, but it is real. . . . People in this town expect an honest day's work." Like Pittsburgh players of the past, today's Pirates are working hard to add a new page to the club's history of baseball excellence.

ZACH DUKE

ZACH DUKE – A big, left-handed hurler, Duke earned league-wide attention by going 8–2 with a 1.81 ERA during his rookie season in 2005. Pittsburgh fans hoped he would help the Pirates continue to rise by improving on his 10-victory performance in 2006.

MANAGER · FRED CLARKE

In 1897, 25-year-old outfielder Fred Clarke was named player/manager of his club, the Louisville Colonels. Despite the added responsibility, Clarke hit a career-best .390 that year. Then, in 1900, Clarke was sent to Pittsburgh to take over the reins of the Pirates. In the Steel City, Clarke continued to star on the field and to drive the Pirates to victory after victory as manager. Clarke's Pittsburgh teams topped the NL four times between 1901 and 1909 and competed in two World Series. Clarke completed his playing career with a .315 lifetime batting average and his managing career with a .576 winning percentage.

STATS

Pirates seasons as player/manager:
   1900–15

Height: 5-10

Weight: 165

Managerial Record: 1,602–1,181

World Series Championship: 1909

Baseball Hall of Fame inductee (1945)

FRED CLARKE
MANAGER

PITTSBURGH
PIRATES